D0338789

The
Great
American
Misf it

Warren G. Harding

The
Great
American
Misf.t
i

26 Bizarre Personal Histories

written and illustrated by
WILLIAM BRAMHALL

with a foreword by
JOHN TRAIN

CLARKSON N. POTTER, INC. / *Publishers, New York*
Distributed by Crown Publishers, Inc.

Copyright © 1982 by William Bramhall, Jr.

All rights reserved. No part of this book may be reproduced or transmitted in any form or by any means, electronic or mechanical, including photocopying, recording, or by any information storage and retrieval system, without permission in writing from the publisher.

Published by Clarkson N. Potter, Inc.,
One Park Avenue, New York, New York 10016, and simultaneously in Canada by General Publishing Company Limited

Manufactured in the United States of America

Library of Congress Cataloging in Publication Data

Bramhall, William.
    The great American misfit.

    1. Eccentrics and eccentricities—United States—
Biography.   2. United States—Biography.   I. Title.
CT9990.B7   1982   920′.073 [B]   82-7692
ISBN: 0-517-54758-9   AACR2

Book design by Katy Homans

10   9   8   7   6   5   4   3   2   1

First Edition

LIBRARY

OCT 6 1983

UNIVERSITY OF THE PACIFIC
411132

To Pamela, with love

Contents

7

Acknowledgments

I would like to acknowledge the encouraging support and sound advice of my editors, Nancy Novogrod and Carol Southern, in the making of this book. My sincere thanks to Ted Riley, agent provocateur, *without whom it would not have been possible.*

Foreword

THERE ARE SOME extraordinary stories in Mr. Bramhall's little book.

Surely the ultimate tale of dubious heirs claiming the estates of well-known plutocrats, from Princess Anastasia to Howard Hughes, is Bramhall's saga of rich, beautiful Ida Mayfield, a Louisiana belle who came north. She rode high in New York society from the Civil War on, marrying a congressman-press-lord, dancing with the Prince of Wales, entertaining one President and snooting another. Then she vanishes. When Ida dies, scores of her Mayfield kinfolk come north to claim their share of the boodle. But the court discovers that Ida, in reality the daughter of an immigrant worker named Walsh, had invented her glamorous background. The "Mayfields" have no claim whatever.

One hopes for a sequel to the volume. A good prospect would be General Wilkinson, Chief of Staff of the American Army during the Napoleonic Wars. He collected not only his official salary but additional secret stipends from the British, the French, and Aaron Burr, whose plan to organize a force to invade Mexico required that the general turn a blind eye. Since Mexico was a possession of Napoleon's empire, his French employers insisted that Burr's expedition be halted. The General grudgingly complied, thus losing a significant part of his income. He was, however, decorated for loyalty.

Somehow the American eccentrics seem more vivid and dramatic than the English ones described in, for instance, Edith Sitwell's delightful *The English Eccentrics*. Also, less graceful. Perhaps the English could afford to be whimsical because they were rich, while Americans have generally had to superimpose their follies on the job of getting there, making for a bumpier course. Still, in this age of flat characters they deserve to be better known, and to that worthy purpose Mr. Bramhall has made a solid contribution.

JOHN TRAIN
May 26, 1982

Introduction

AMERICANS HAVE ALWAYS felt a compulsion to destroy
their heroes. Psychiatrists tell us that this is because the or-
dinary man, in tearing down his hero, builds himself up.
This strikes me as implausible. For one thing, it assumes
that we are pleased enough with our heroes to feel inferior
to them. I suspect a more mundane motive. The reason we
destroy our heroes is because we are, in fact, bored by
them. Heroes, let's hear it said, are as bland as oatmeal. In
destroying them, we are like the little boy, who displeased
with the tasteless contents of his breakfast bowl, upends it
on the table. It's really that simple. From childhood on, we
are spooned a tepid pablum of wise presidents, brilliant sci-
entists, fearless generals, fearless baseball players, until finally something snaps. Out of sheer ennui, we upend the
golden bowl.

I believe that the only way to avoid becoming bored
by the heroic, and thereby destroying it, is to develop the
cult of the unheroic. Hence, this book. Around the star-
spangled banner I tried to embroider a fringe of bright and
many colored hues. One might call it a lunatic fringe.
Strolling along the banks of the big muddy river of American history, I looked not toward the main current, but into
the placid backwashes and obscure side eddies, where, in
the warm and still waters, dark and exotic life-forms pro-
create. Sometimes, as in the case of a George Armstrong
Custer or a Warren G. Harding, these rare specimens are
swept out into the mainstream, there to bob briefly and
sink, but for the most part the individuals you will encoun-
ter here do not appear in the standard texts. History has
forgotten them, and with good reason.

You will not find Ann Putnam's likeness among Norman

Rockwell's portraits of quaint village life, nor is it likely that a movie will ever be made about the frontier career of Stephen Meek. There is no portico in the baseball Hall of Fame honoring Chick Gandil. James A. Harden-Hickey's magnum opus is long out of print and with any luck will remain so. You will search in vain for any mention of Wilbur Glenn Voliva or "Dr." John Brinkley in a *Who's Who in Science*. Yet each left his mark on American life, as surely as a kid with a candy bar will leave his mark on your sofa. On the tabula rasa that was the New World, some came not to write their names but to drag their fingers across the slate. Here are their stories.

The
Great
American
Misf t

i

Ann Putnam

Ann Putnam

IN 1692 IN SALEM, MASSACHUSETTS, there lived a little girl named Ann Putnam, who had an unusually active imagination. In those days children had to amuse themselves with games of their own invention and Ann liked to pretend that the neighbors were witches out to get her. What made the game especially exciting was that the grown-ups actually believed her. To Ann's delighted amazement they brought the witches into court and even had them punished. Her friends asked if they could play too and the witch hunt spread. Soon citizens from surrounding towns were being dragged into Salem to face the accusing children. And that was just the beginning. Before the witch hunt was through, 150 people were thrown in jail, countless others fled, their property confiscated, and the limbs of the great oak on Gallows Hill creaked from the hanging weight of 13 women, 6 men, and 2 dogs.

Ann's victims were young and old, rich and poor, black and white. Even a minister trudged prayerfully up the scaffold steps on her say-so. Unlike more recent witch hunters, she didn't discriminate. She was, however, influenced by her mother, who saw in the situation an opportunity both to cleanse the community of devils and to settle some old scores with the neighbors. The legal conventions of the day also worked in Ann's favor. Those who pleaded innocent were summarily hanged, their very plea being evidence against them, while those who pleaded guilty were pardoned if they named more witches for the judges. When an accused witch appeared in court to protest her innocence, Ann and the other girls countered with an ingenious forensic tactic. They barked like dogs. They fell down in a heap. They rolled on the floor like "beef creatures." "There was little occasion to prove witchcraft," wrote Calvinist ideologue Cotton Mather, "this being evident and notorious to all beholders."

As fear swept like the wind through the colony, 12-year-old Ann became a celebrity. When Andover was stricken with a witch problem, the sibylic moppet was imported as a visiting consultant. Greeted by the wonder-struck populace like a foreign princess, she bestowed upon them her gifts of panic, paranoia, and mass hysteria, and left with the jails crammed to capacity.

But it was not to last. When Governor Phips's wife was "cried out" on, he suspended the trials and ordered new rules of evidence drawn up. Hallucinations were no longer admissable and Ann was not allowed to testify, much to the disappointment of her parents, who foresaw, with Delphic prescience, a complete collapse of family prestige.

Lord Cornbury

THOSE WHO FRET THAT today's well-dressed man might wear rouge should know there is nothing new in this. The tradition goes back almost three hundred years to the then governor of New York, Lord Cornbury. In fact, Cornbury did today's male one better. He also wore a dress.

The colonists of 1702 were excited about the appointment of Edward Hyde, Viscount Cornbury, as their next governor general. The eldest son of the Earl of Clarendon and a cousin of Queen Anne, he was thought to possess valuable access to the crown. The morning after he arrived in New York, a delegation of chamber of commerce types was sent to officially welcome him. Their enthusiasm turned to dismay as they came into view of the Governor's residence. Sitting on the front porch, rocking back and forth and tatting a lace doily, was Cornbury dressed

Lord Cornbury

from head to toe in one of his wife's gowns. Exchanging worried looks, the colonists tiptoed back to their houses.

More surprises were in store when Cornbury threw his first dress ball. Attired in a simply gorgeous Régence sacque gown, he graciously greeted his guests and then astounded them by charging an admission fee. Next, he insisted they all file past his wife and feel, of all things, her ears, which he compared to "conch shells" in a long poem he had written. The colonists, all practical burghers and merchants, did their best to remain polite. Smiles were hidden behind fans, buckled shoes nudged hosed shins under the tables. He was, after all, a cousin of the Queen's. In fact, he was a bit of a queen himself.

Their smiles vanished when they learned Cornbury's real purpose in seeking colonial appointment was to escape creditors in England. They decided to keep a close eye on him and their vigilance was rewarded. In 1708 he was caught red-handed embezzling public funds designated for the construction of a fort. He had even started to build a house for himself with the stolen money. Insult was added to injury when Lady Cornbury, she of the perfect ears, was also found to be a thief. It seems she stole dresses from the local aristocracy, replenishing a wardrobe no doubt depleted by her husband's appetites.

Cornbury was thrown into debtor's prison and remained there until the death of his father allowed him to inherit his title and return to England. There are no monuments erected to the memory of Edward Hyde, Viscount Cornbury, though he did leave his family name on a tract of land on the Hudson. It is called Hyde Park.

General Horatio Gates

AS ONE OF THE CONTINENTAL army's most incompetent officers, General Horatio Gates was living proof of Talleyrand's maxim that war is too serious a thing to be left to military men. When Gates let slip the dogs of war, they usually turned around and bit him.

Gates joined the American army after being passed over for promotion in the British. He was, if nothing else, ambitious. By 1777 he had connived his way into commanding the patriot troops in the Saratoga campaign. At the pivotal battle of Bemis Heights, Gates was too involved in a political debate with a captured British major to notice that his own subordinate officers had routed the enemy forces. He then nearly plucked defeat from the jaws of victory by negotiating a surrender treaty that allowed the British army to return to England if they promised never to come back. These terms were immediately revoked by an alarmed Congress.

Gates always resented the choice of George Washington as Commander in Chief. While Washington's wooden teeth chattered in Valley Forge, Gates tried to convince Congress that he was a better man for the job. Though frustrated, he did get the next best thing—command of the Southern War Department. Here at last was his chance to put to rest a reputation for excessive caution. No more would the enemy call him the Old Midwife. No more would his own troops call him Granny Gates. At the Battle of Camden, he would take the offensive.

Fortune may favor the bold but rarely does it favor the stupid. After a forced march across miles of barren, hostile territory, which reduced his men to eating unripened corn, Gates gave them a ration of molasses instead of their usual tot of rum. The entire army came down with diarrhea. In this miserable condition it blundered first into a swamp and then into Lord Corn-

General Horatio Gates

wallis's seasoned grenadiers. Incapable of giving orders, Gates watched in stunned silence as two-thirds of his troops fled panic-stricken without firing a shot. Then he about-faced and galloped 200 miles in less than 48 hours. "It does admirable credit to the activity of a man at his time of life," remarked a sarcastic Alexander Hamilton.

After Camden, Congress decided it had had enough of General Gates and stripped him of his command.

Captain Alden Partridge

THOSE WHO CANNOT DO, teach, as the old saying goes, and those who cannot teach, teach at West Point, as the career of Alden Parrridge proves.

Partridge was hired by the academy in 1807, his only military experience being as a cadet himself. That the cadets took an immediate liking to him was not a good sign at a place like West Point. On sunny mornings he would lead his student warriors into the fields for a drawing lesson. The afternoons might be spent learning French. A true fair-weather soldier, Partridge could always be counted on to cancel the artillery drill when it rained, and best of all he gave no examinations. The only test a cadet had to face was whether or not "Old Pewt" liked him, and he liked almost anybody who agreed with him. The effectiveness of the Partridge pedagogy was measured during the War of 1812 when ragbag American armies fired on each other by mistake, got lost in the Canadian woods, and allowed British forces a fraction of their size to burn down Washington.

To the delight of the young republic's enemies, Partridge was appointed Superintendent in 1815. He ran West Point as a family franchise. An uncle was put in charge of the mess, a nephew was installed as post adjutant, and yet another relative ran the cadet store, where he returned a handsome profit in uniforms. Old Pewt continued to graduate only those cadets whose flattery had pleased him. Cadets who were especially sycophantic were given vacation leave with full academic credit, a privilege enjoyed by nearly half the corps. When the other faculty members complained to President Monroe of Partridge's "ruinous tendencies," he arrested them and taught all the classes himself.

In 1817 it was decided that Partridge had to be replaced, but this proved easier said than done. Partridge fomented a cadet mutiny against the officer who had been sent to relieve him and was court-martialed for insubordination. The rest of his life was spent reigning over an obscure military academy in Norwich, Vermont, lobbying for the abolition of his former fiefdom on the Hudson.

Captain Alden Partridge

Stephen Meek

Stephen Meek

"Go west, young man," advised Horace Greeley, but then he didn't know about scouts like Stephen Meek.

In the spring of 1845, Meek persuaded a large, oxen-drawn wagon train to depart the Oregon Trail at Fort Boise, claiming that he knew a shortcut that would take them west. The emigrants didn't know that Meek was a friend of Lansford Hastings, the man who sold the map to the Donner Party, and it took them nearly a week to realize their mistake.

Progress had slowed to a crawl. The oxen were lowing in pain as they gingerly picked their way over the stony lunar landscape of Oregon's high desert. Many of the prairie schooners had foundered on the boulder-strewn wastes. This was some shortcut. Thinking better late than never, they approached Meek and demanded to be taken back to Fort Boise. It was then they heard the really bad news. Meek had no idea where he was. Too ashamed to tell them, he had been lost for days.

"Like mariners at sea," as one of them dolorously described it, they wandered about the pelagic expanses of sand, scrub, and sticker patches that stretched in every direction. The heat became infernal as spring turned to summer. At one point they remained stationary for five days at a mudhole, not knowing where the next source of water lay. Provisions ran low and the pioneers had to eat their cattle. There was an outbreak of camp fever that claimed many lives. Week followed blistering week.

Anger, grief, and resentment began to simmer under the terrible sun. There was talk of stringing Meek up, and few of the emigrants came forward to defend him. Even one of his sympathizers wrote that "his head will not be worth a chew of tobacco to him." However, Meek's life was spared when the lynching party was unable to find a tree.

After nearly two months in the wilderness, the biblical travail of the lost wagon train reached a climax when the frontier Moses deserted his flock. As if a curse had been lifted, a relief party arrived soon thereafter and led the travelers to safety.

For several years, the Meek Cutoff remained the basis of a macabre joke among Oregon-bound pioneers, who told each other how "it came pretty near cuttin' off those who tried it."

Kit Burns

LET US TRAVEL BACK in time and visit Sportsmen's Hall, Kit Burns proprietor. It is a vaporous evening in 1850. The place is Manhattan's tough-as-nails Fourth Ward. We walk through streets flanked by old Knickerbocker houses that have long since crumbled into slums. Turning down Water Street, we come to a door painted a bright, bilious green. After repeated knocking, it opens like a maw.

Inside is a churning sea of sweating, swearing, shouting humanity. The din is deafening. The focus of the turmoil is a large pit surrounded by bleachers and presided over by Kit Burns himself. Furiously, bets are placed as Kit lets loose a wharf rat the size of a raccoon. Cheers. He unleashes a terrior. More cheers. The fur flies. Shrieks, both human and animal, rise to a fever pitch. The terrier pants, staggers, falls, and a roar fills Sportsmen's Hall.

More murine entertainment is provided by Kit's son-in-law, Jack the Rat. Jumping into the pit, he offers to bite off the head of a live mouse for a dime. For a quarter he will decapitate his own namesake. Take that, Beatrix Potter!

Kit Burns

A man is known by the company he keeps and Kit Burns's character is reflected in his clientele. In the first row of bleachers sits Hell Cat Marie, bedazzled with razors that gleam in the gaslight. The ends of her fingers are adorned with brass claws. Beside her is Slobbery Jim, wearing the same hobnail boots in which he had stomped Patsy the Barber to death. Conspicuous also is Snatchem, self-described as a "rough-and-tumble-stand-up-to-be-knocked-down-son-of-a-gun-kicking-in-the-head-knife-in-a-dark-room fellow." He claimed he wanted to go to heaven so he could "bite off Gabriel's ear."

A fistfight breaks out between Sow Madden and Cowlegged Sam McCarthy, but it doesn't last long. Arriving to break it up is the bouncer, a minatory female named Gallus Mag after the "galluses" holding up her pantaloons. After subduing Sam with a belaying pin, she obliges the cheering crowd by chewing off his ear.

The merriment lasts until dawn. The next day is Sunday and Kit decides to get some good publicity by allowing a prayer meeting in Sportsmen's Hall. It is not mentioned in the newspaper account of the gathering that the evangelists are charged $150 rent, or that while praying for Kit's soul, they hold their noses against the fetid stench of decomposing dog and rodent bones scattered under the temporary pews.

William Walker

SINCE BOYHOOD IN TENNESSEE, William Walker had dreamed of having his own Latin American country to rule. The first attempt to achieve that dream came in 1853 after he failed to strike a claim in the Gold Rush. Recruiting a handful of supporters from the bars of San Francisco, he launched an armed invasion of Baja California. He had just enough time to proclaim himself President before the Mexican police arrived and escorted him across the border. He was advised not to return.

Two years later Walker enlisted as a mercenary in one of the factions fighting a civil war in Nicaragua and hit the jackpot. By a combination of military recklessness and the kind of good fortune that can attend the disreputable, he captured the capital city of Granada, deposed the president, and named himself dictator.

His rule was not popular. Among his first edicts was a decree reinstituting slavery, abolished thirty years before. Unable to speak Spanish, he declared that English was the official language of the nation. Then he began bestowing land grants on his friends from Alabama and Louisiana and, in a megalomaniacal frenzy, seized the Accessory Transit Company, Cornelius Vanderbilt's trade link to the Pacific markets.

The latter proved to be a fatal blunder, for the irate Commodore organized an army, which recaptured the Transit Line and surrounded Walker in Granada. He finally gave up, but not before his followers had destroyed the city in a drunken looting spree. He was shipped back to New Orleans, where in the Mardi Gras spirit half the town turned out to welcome him as a conquering hero.

Uncle Bill, as he became known in the saloons of the French Quarter, attempted three more invasions of Central America, none meeting with the success of his earlier coup and the last

29

William Walker

ending in his execution by a Honduran firing squad in 1860 before a crowd of cheering natives. His name is still invoked by Nicaraguan parents as a *yanqui* bogeyman who devours disobedient children.

Henry Clubb

UTOPIAN THEORIES HAVE ENJOYED a long, inane history in America. Take octagonism, for example, the belief that eight-sided houses promote domestic tranquillity and spiritual harmony. Or take Henry Clubb, who combined the precepts of octagonism with those of vegetarianism and then applied both to an entire metropolis.

Octagon City came to Henry Clubb in a vision in 1856. It was a vision of a city rising from the plain, a city at whose center stood a Parnassian Grand Octagon. Surrounding it were hundreds of satellite octagons, each on an eight-sided lot. The fields were swollen with corn; oceans of rye waved in the breeze. The octagonal vegetable plots overflowed with tomatoes the size of basketballs, turgid turnips, Brobdingnagian broccoli. Happy, healthy farmers shared food and song. With a clarity known only by fanatics, Henry Clubb was convinced that he could make the dream come true.

He founded the Vegetarian Settlement Company to sell stock in Octagon City. A brochure described the new Eldorado rising on the banks of the Neosho River in Kansas Territory, the sawmill a-sawing, the gristmill a-grinding, the settlers pouring in. Among those who read and believed and went was a family named Colt.

As Mrs. Colt tells it, only a sod-roof cabin and miles upon miles of bare open prairie greeted the Octo-vegetarians when they arrived. There was no Grand Octagon, no sawmill, no gristmill. The only mill that appeared to be working was Clubb's publicity mill. Most of the emigrants took one look around and headed back east, but the Colt family decided to stick it out.

In between dust storms and prairie fires they scratched a meager living from the hardpan. Periodically, the sky was blackened by rain clouds that flooded their crops or locusts that ate them. Under the onslaught of nature, Clubb's geometric fantasy gradually crumbled. The settlers saw less and less of him until finally he appeared only on Sunday to preach a sermon. Then he vanished, no one knew where. By October the Colts had had it and made the long trek back east. Mr. Colt died en route.

When Mrs. Colt's *Went to Kansas, Being a Thrilling Account of an Ill Fated Expedition to that Fairy Land and Its Sad Results* was published, it threw cold water on Octagon City. Emigration, at its highest no more than a trickle, ceased entirely. The sod-roof cabin was slowly reclaimed by the wind and rain, and after a few years Octagon City was no more than a bad memory. No one knows what became of Henry Clubb.

Henry Clubb

Ida Mayfield

Ida Mayfield

DURING THE CIVIL WAR, New York society was dazzled by a peaches-and-cream belle from Louisiana named Ida Mayfield. She made a lasting impression on the city, where Southern sentiment ran high, by snubbing President Lincoln when he came to campaign. She was bold and beautiful and no one was surprised when she married Ben Wood, copperhead congressman and newspaper publisher. After the war, the Woods rode the crest of the social wave, a real life Scarlett and Rhett. Ben showered Ida with jewels. She was presented to Empress Eugénie. She danced with the Prince of Wales. She entertained President Cleveland. Then came the panic of 1907 and Ida mysteriously vanished.

In 1931 a ninety-four-year-old hermit was discovered in the Herald Square Hotel, an ancient edifice squeezed in between the emerging skyscrapers. No one knew how long she had lived there. Her room looked like a hamster's cage. There were mountains of yellowed newspapers. Hundreds of letters covered the floor. A wild assortment of cartons, boxes, and trunks were stacked from floor to ceiling. Through the Havishamian rubbish shuffled a shrunken, blind, deaf old woman wearing two hotel towels pinned together for a dress, with skin as smooth as porcelain.

Ida was judged to be incompetent and appointed a ward of the court. Then the fun began. The prying hands of the law opened the cardboard boxes and unwrapped the mummified parcels. Inside were negotiable securities worth hundreds of thousands of dollars. Thousands more in cash were found nestled in frying pans and crumbling shoeboxes. A diamond-and-emerald necklace was squirreled away in a box of crackers. The real treasure, discovered by a nurse, was tied around Ida's waist. Inside a canvas-and-oilcloth pouch were fifty ten-thousand-dollar bills. When they took this from her, Ida died.

Scores of Mayfields tramped up from Louisiana to claim the fortune, filling the probate court thicker than mosquitoes in a bayou. When they heard what the judge had to say, several of them fainted.

Ida Mayfield had never existed.

The woman who claimed to be Ida Mayfield was actually Ellen Walsh, an impoverished daughter of an immigrant textile worker. She had invented the belle from New Orleans fiction to open doors, and with the help of a borrowed dress, it had worked. Ida Mayfield was a name she had made up. Not even Ben Wood had known the truth.

Crestfallen, the Mayfield clan dispersed. Ellen Walsh's estate was distributed among the handful of her descendants who could be located. They had no idea their ancestor had ever lived.

George Armstrong Custer

In 1861, GEORGE ARMSTRONG CUSTER graduated from West Point at the bottom of his class. It made no difference to his career. Custer had something more valuable than brains or talent. Custer had luck.

During the Civil War he had the good fortune to serve under Phil Sheridan, and while Custer had no more strategic sense than a staghound, Sheridan had it to spare. What Sheridan needed was an officer with reckless, preferably suicidal disregard for danger. Custer filled the bill. His love of battle was as juvenile as Tom Sawyer's. The smell of black powder was like angel dust in his nostrils. He quite speedily carved a reputation as the Union's fiercest cavalry commander, a Genghis Khan in blue velveteen. A score of horses were shot from under him. At age twenty-three

George Armstrong Custer

he became the youngest brigadier general in American history.

"Custer's Luck" became a military byword. After the war the boy general was again assigned to his old commander. Although Custer was often insubordinate, Sheridan overlooked it. "Youth is high-spirited," he would say. He also said, "The only good Indian is a dead Indian." Custer was ordered to make good on the remark.

The pinnacle of his Indian fighting was the Washita Massacre. One snowy winter's dawn, seven hundred of his men surrounded a slumbering Cheyenne village and opened fire. Even if they had been awake, the Cheyenne would have been surprised: they had just signed a peace treaty with the government. But the victory had a smudge on it. Twenty of Custer's men were missing and he made no effort to search for them. They were later found frozen solid as TV dinners. There was talk of an investigation but no action was taken. Custer's luck held.

Until June 25, 1876. On that morning, he led six hundred men of the Seventh Cavalry into the valley of the Little Bighorn, and for once in his life he was at the wrong place at the wrong time. Typically, he was disobeying orders. Typically, he hadn't reconnoitered. Typically, he was so excited that it was difficult to understand what he was saying. "Hold your horses, boys," he piped in his high, shrill voice, "there's plenty down there for all of us." Four thousand Sioux said, "Right you are."

Boston Corbett

IN 1865 A HAT MAKER and religious fanatic named Boston Corbett shot John Wilkes Booth after a squadron of federal troops trapped the American Brutus in a burning barn. The order to fire

Boston Corbett

had come not from his commanding officer, who wanted to take Booth alive, but from God.

Heavenly dicta were a frequent occurrence in Corbett's life and had produced something of a hair-trigger temperament. Some years earlier, while street preaching in the city whose name he had borrowed, he was eyed salaciously by two prostitutes. Obeying the voice from above, Corbett went home and castrated himself.

When he enlisted in the Army of the Potomac, his habit of bellowing forth hymns or staring silently at what he claimed were lights in the sky made him a mystery to his companions, but they all agreed he was a hellion in battle. During the fight at Culpeper Court House, he held twenty-six of Mosby's Rangers at bay single-handed before being captured. The five months he spent in Andersonville Prison cannot have had a tranquilizing effect on his volatile personality.

After killing Booth, Corbett billed himself the Avenger of Blood and was in great demand on the lecture circuit, but bookings declined when it became known he strayed from his topic to lambaste his audience with direct messages from Jehovah.

By 1886 he had wandered out to Kansas where he was pensioned off as a doorkeeper to the state legislature, an assembly he prorogued one spring day by emptying the contents of two revolvers into its midst. Fortunately, no one was hurt, and though Corbett insisted he was acting on orders from You Know Who, he was remanded to the Topeka Asylum for the Insane. It wasn't long before he escaped, leaving behind a message addressed to the American people complaining of public ingratitude for his services. He was never heard from again.

Hetty Green

ACCORDING TO THE *Guinness Book of World Records*, the greatest miser who ever lived was Hetty Howland Robinson Green. How stingy was she? In 1886, when her son injured his leg, multimillionaire Hetty disguised herself as a pauper and dragged him through the charity wards, attempting to get free medical attention. The delay in proper treatment resulted in amputation.

Hetty's financial career began at the age of six when she read the financial pages to her whaling captain father. When her aunt died, Hetty committed perjury and forgery to get the lion's share of the estate. She then astounded Wall Street by managing the money herself. Lending it out at high interest—Collis P. Huntington called her "nothing more than a glorified pawnbroker"—she soon had $91,000,000 worth of pennies to pinch.

And pinch them she did. She saved on laundry detergent by washing only the lower portions of her skirts and wore her black dresses until they turned brown and then green with age. She lived in a cold-water walk-up in the slums of Hoboken. She once stayed up half the night searching for a lost two penny postage stamp. After she finished reading the paper, she sent her son hobbling off on his cork leg to resell it. When she married Edward Green, an affable soul wealthy in his own right, she made him sign a contract forsaking any claim to her estate. They were separated when Hetty became disgusted with his bungled investments.

As a favored customer, Hetty was given a free office at the Chemical Bank. The clerks trembled like Dickens characters whenever she came in. Wrapped in a tattered talma and crowned with a moldering bonnet, the "Witch of Wall Street" swept into the bank vaults like some crepuscular apparition, the keys to safe-deposit boxes clanking under the folds of rotting fabric. For

41

Hetty Green

hours she would sit on the cold marble floor, fingering her notes and certificates. At lunchtime she would heat up some oatmeal on the radiator or munch a cracker, the crumbs spilling down her front.

In a life vacant of charitable works, the only creature known to be the object of a Hetty Green kindness was a baleful Skye terrier named Cutey Dewey after the Admiral. The coddled canine dined off pheasant and grouse that would have made Edward VII's mouth water. Hetty's death, of a stroke sustained while arguing food costs with a cook, was not widely mourned.

Ned Green

HETTY'S SON DID NOT INHERIT her respect for money. Ned Green, a 6-foot-4-inch, 300-pound, cork-legged behemoth, was as profligate as his mother was parsimonious.

As a young man Ned was sent to Texas to manage one of Hetty's railroads. No sooner did Momma turn her back than he was riding about in a private Pullman car named *Mabel* after a Chicago prostitute. Gone were the days of childhood, when he had been hauled to school in a cart, his clothes stuffed with newspapers to keep out the cold.

When Hetty died in 1916, Ned really cut loose. He built a mansion in the ancestral town of New Bedford, Massachusetts, and infuriated the neighbors by mooring a dirigible overhead. Mabel was installed as mistress of the house, but sad to say, she was not the Duchess of Marlborough. Before long she was spending the day in bed with the gardener, the delivery boy, the pastry chef, the valet, even the butler.

Ned didn't care. He had terminal ennui. Though he sat on the boards of several corporations, the only motion he ever made was to adjourn. Of far greater interest to him was his pornography collection, the largest in the world, and his yacht, also the largest in the world. His seafaring ancestors must have spun like tops in their graves when he sank it in sixteen feet of water in Buzzards Bay.

Ned was as sedentary as a pasha. For hours he would paw over his stamp collection, his coin collection, his jewelry collection, his jigsaw-puzzle collection, his slot-machine collection, and—most precious of all—his collection of young female "wards." There were twenty-four of these nubile maidens gamboling about the estate—chambermaids, farmers' daughters, child actresses. It was Ned's idea to put them through Wellesley, but most flunked out.

His last years were spent in Star Island, Florida, where he threw gala parties on a Mississippi showboat. Ned rarely showed himself at the fetes, preferring, like Gatsby, to hide in his room and watch the hundreds of strangers eat his food, drink his champagne, and dance to his music under the Japanese lanterns.

In 1936, he started another collection with the purchase of a fourteen-foot-long whale's penis for $1,700. Mercifully, death put an end to this new mania. "This really is a beautiful country, isn't it?" he said before he died. "I just wish I could stay around a little longer. You know, some of it's been fun."

Ned Green

Sarah Winchester

$\mathcal{S}arah$ $\mathcal{W}inchester$

SARAH WINCHESTER'S PROBLEM was ghosts, lots of them. As heir to the Winchester Arms fortune, Sarah believed she was haunted by the spirits of those killed by the "gun that won the West." What was she to do? To find the answer, she visited a medium in Boston. The spirits would be placated, said the medium, if Sarah provided a home for them. As long as she kept building it, the ghosts wouldn't hurt her.

So in 1884, Sarah bought an eight-room house in San Jose, California. It did not remain an eight-room house for long. It grew to twenty rooms, then forty, then sixty. A hundred rooms, and still it grew. It spread over the flats like a Victorian ginger-bread version of the Blob. Surrounding buildings were engulfed as if by osmosis. For thirty-eight years a crew of twenty carpenters worked day and night on the dilative house. It eventually rose to a height of seven stories and covered six acres. Servants needed maps to find their way about the 160-room rabbit warren, with its two thousand doors, ten thousand windows, forty staircases, and six kitchens.

Sarah employed no architects to help her. Each night at the stroke of twelve, a bell summoned the spirits to a séance room, and a design conference was held. The ghostly taste soon became evident. Because ghosts like to enter through chimneys, they insisted there be plenty of these. Sarah built forty-seven. Because ghosts are frightened by their own reflections, they demanded there be few mirrors. There were only two. Because ghosts like the number thirteen, they wanted it used as a design motif. It appeared everywhere, most notably in the thirteen bathrooms, the thirteenth of which had thirteen windows and thirteen steps leading up to it.

Everyone knows ghosts like practical jokes. On the second story a door was installed that opened on to nothing but thin air.

Another opened to reveal a blank wall. Staircases climbed to the ceiling and stopped. Passageways were only two feet wide. One closet was the size of a three-bedroom apartment; another was only one-inch deep. A skylight was stuck in the middle of the floor. Newel posts were installed upside down.

Only Sarah's death at age eighty-one put an end to the clamor of hammer and saw. The present owners of the Winchester House do not share her regard for spirits. They have converted several of the rooms into the Winchester Rifle Museum which depicts in wax-figure dioramas the story of the gun that started it all.

Al Jennings

IN HIS AUTOBIOGRAPHY, *Beating Back*, Al Jennings claimed to have killed dozens of men. This is unlikely. For one thing, he was a notoriously bad shot. For another, his outlaw career lasted less than three months and was as unsuccessful as it was brief.

During his first train robbery attempt in 1885, Jennings was almost killed when the locomotive smashed through the barricade he had built on the tracks. For his second attempt, he galloped alongside the train firing a sixshooter in the air, but the engineer waved cheerfully at him and sped on. His third effort met with partial success—he actually stopped the train, but when he tried to blow up the safe, he used too much dynamite and the mail car, loot and all, was blasted to smithereens. To make matters worse, his mask slipped down and he was recognized immediately. Three days later he meekly surrendered to a sheriff who

Al Jennings

had wagered another lawman that he could capture Jennings without firing a shot.

Jennings was pardoned after serving five years of a fifty-year sentence, everyone agreeing that he was a threat more to himself than to society. He became a permanent fixture at rodeos and old timers' barbecues, celebrated for wild stories about his life in crime. He even starred in an early western movie, which was shot in a small town. The citizens angrily attacked Jennings as he "robbed" the bank, unaware that it was only make-believe. Even as a celluloid outlaw he was hapless.

In 1942, at the age of eighty-five, Jennings was still shooting off his mouth, if no longer his gun. In a feeble publicity ploy, 101-year-old Frank Dalton had claimed to be Jesse James and Jennings came forth to identify him. "Yessir, that's Jesse," he said, "no doubt about it." He was delighted that the wire services carried a photograph of the two ancient desperadoes pointing Colt revolvers at the camera. When not involved in harebrained publicity stunts, Jennings raised chickens in a suburb of Los Angeles. He died in 1962 at the ripe old age of ninety-eight.

James A. Harden-Hickey

IT IS SOMETIMES SAID that everyone has at least one book in him. Thankfully, most of these are never written, but no such luck with James A. Harden-Hickey, whose *Euthanasia, the Aesthetics of Suicide* was published by the Truth Seeker Publishing Company in 1894. *Euthanasia* was a do-it-yourself manual for the terminally inclined. Harden-Hickey wrote it in the library of his father-in-law, the steel tycoon John Flagler, who had always suspected him of being a fop but now saw far worse fears realized. The book consisted mainly of quotations "by the greatest thinkers the world has ever produced," which were carefully selected to promote and encourage self-annihilation. A sampler:

"The wise man lives as long as he ought, not as long as he can."
"Nature is kind and considerate in giving us the power of dying; there are a thousand ways out of life, though but one way into it."
"Death is a cure not of one but of every evil, a harbor never to be feared, often to be sought."
"The best way never to fear death is always to be thinking about it."

There exists a consensus among the collectors of curiosa that these quotations were almost entirely spurious and the product of Harden-Hickey's own morbid imagination. All in all a total of fifty-one lethal instruments and eighty-three poisons were recommended as being particularly efficient. Several of the *modi morendi* were accompanied by grim illustrations.

Harden-Hickey had more than just literary ambitions. The same year his book was published, he took advantage of a provision in international law and proclaimed himself king of an uninhabited island seven hundred miles off the coast of Brazil. He

James A. Harden-Hickey

even opened a chancellery on Thirty-second Street, sparsely furnished with one table, three chairs, and an oilcloth carpet. When Great Britain seized the island for a coaling station, Harden-Hickey became livid and vented his rage in a series of letters to the State Department. The illegible letters were ignored. After failing to persuade his father-in-law to finance an invasion of England, Harden-Hickey practiced what he preached, his own death resulting from an overdose of chloral, self-administered in an El Paso hotel room. In his suitcase was discovered a home-made crown.

Zeo Zoe Wilkins

IN 1903, ZEO ZOE WILKINS commenced a matrimonial career remarkable even by today's standards. Her first husband was a fellow student at osteopathy college. The bride blushingly opened her heart to a girl friend: "I shall get enough money to finance my start in osteopathy and then divorce him." When she did precisely that, the overwrought young man committed suicide.

Mourning was brief for Zeo Zoe and it wasn't long before wedding bells were again ringing for the girl with the Dr. Seuss name. Her second husband was a San Antonio bone manipulator whom she pumped full of lead when he stumbled in on an extra-marital affair she was conducting in their parlor. Batting her eyes, she told the police that she thought he was a burglar.

Publicity surrounded her like perfume. She had more suitors than Penelope on Ithaca. First in line was a banker, whose bank failed when he was caught embezzling funds for his *inamorata*.

53

Next was a chemist, gunned down in a street fight. "He gave me all his money and went to get more, poor man," eulogized Zeo Zoe in her diary. Next was a furniture dealer, who lavished pearls and furs upon her and was arrested trying to steal more. The next bee to fall into the flower was seventy-two-year-old T. W. Cunningham. Before his friends had the marriage annulled on grounds that he was insane, Zeo Zoe had wrung a half-million-dollar settlement out of his estate. Her next husband was T.W.'s chauffeur. They too were divorced, this time because of a macabre joke she sprang on him. He did not think the mock suicide she staged in their nuptial bower was funny.

With this last prankish gesture, Zeo Zoe bid farewell to the world of men and their problems. The Twenties had begun to roar and the dream of having her own osteopathy practice was within her grasp at last. She set up shop in Kansas City and throughout the whoopee years the clinic thrived. And why not? Zeo Zoe blackmailed her patients after she had won their confidence. Some paid. Others chose suicide. Finally there was one who would do neither. When she was found slain in her professional office, the crime made front-page news in several states. Police interviewed scores of people with ample motive, but to this day Zeo Zoe's murder remains unsolved.

Zeo Zoe Wilkins

Joshua II

Joshua II

IN 1906, CORVALLIS, OREGON, was visited by the prophet Joshua II. The menfolk were suspicious. He sure looked an awful lot like that Franz Creffield feller who had been kicked out of the Salvation Army two years earlier for jumping into bed with a woman he was trying to reform. But the local wives and daughters would hear no criticism of Joshua. Why, not only was he a prophet, they said, he was also searching for the Mother of the Second Messiah and Corvallis was where he expected to find her.

The ladies neglected to inform their men how the quest was conducted. After much Bible thumping and speaking in tongues, Joshua would shout, "Vile clothes, be gone!" Then he would personally "examine" the candidates. Small wonder he was so popular. The cult grew so large it had to move to an island in the Willamette River. Across the water in Corvallis the laundry went unwashed, the dinners uncooked, the vegetable plots untended.

One day, someone got close enough to take a Brownie snapshot of one of the evangelical love feasts. The photograph was well frayed by the time it had made the rounds of Corvallis's barbershops and saloons. "Get the tar and feathers!" howled the men, and that very night Joshua was ridden out of town on a rail. Predictably, it solved nothing. The sight of the prophet dripping in molten pitch excited such sympathy among the women that he found himself more popular than ever. In fact, he had become a martyr.

It wasn't long before he flexed his spiritual muscle. When San Francisco was destroyed by an earthquake, Joshua claimed personal responsibility for the disaster and said that Corvallis was next. As if a plug had been pulled, the town drained itself of its female population. Lemming-like, they fled to a Garden of Eden that Joshua had established on a remote strand of beach to take up holy-rolling in the sand. All clothing was burned in a bonfire.

By the light of the flames, Joshua announced that the quest for the Mother was over. The modern Madonna was Esther Mitchell, age seventeen.

But in Corvallis, Esther's colossal brother George joined an armed posse. Tracking Joshua to Portland, George placed a bullet squarely in the prophet's ear as he was weighing himself in front of Quick's Drugstore. The story has a melodramatic ending. The public sentiment was that George had performed a service for the community, and he was acquitted. But as he was boarding the train home, his own ear was pierced by a bullet. The gun that killed him, a pearl-handled derringer, was held by his sister Esther.

Chick Gandil

CHICAGO WHITE SOX first baseman Chick Gandil had the perfect personality for ruining the national pastime. A wild, raw-boned bruiser from the West, Gandil's baseball career began in the outlaw leagues of Texas, where he also moonlighted as a prizefighter in the border town cantinas. When he reached the big leagues, his claw-hammer paws made him a terror at first base and *persona non grata* at hotels. He punched holes in the doors and dropped furniture from the windows. He was as popular with his teammates, who refused to rescue him when he was attacked by opposing players, as he was with his manager, who once tried to strangle him.

In 1919, the White Sox made it to the World Series. Gandil wondered if something more than peanuts and Cracker Jacks could be sold. His ball club, for example. He asked some gam-

Chick Gandil

blers he knew if they'd be interested in making a purchase. They would. He asked his teammates if they'd be interested in throwing the Series. Well, uh, what was in it for them? Why, ten grand each, said Chick. Okay, they said, let's have the money. Later, said Chick.

So the underdog Cincinnati Reds beat the White Sox, and people who knew about the fix made a killing. However, the only player to get rich was Gandil. Telling his teammates that the gamblers had refused to pay him, he kept the bribes for himself. If there is little honor among thieves, there is none among thieving athletes.

"Play Bail!" was the cry heard in the sandlots when the "Black Sox Scandal" broke a year later. The parade of witnesses at the trial might have leaped out of the typewriter of Damon Runyon: sharp-lapel gamblers like Big Bankroll Rothstein and Sleepy Bill Burns, hayseed ballplayers like "Shoeless Joe" Jackson, shyster lawyers like Mouthpiece Fallon, a judge whose remarks included, "Don't get caught off base with that cross-examination, counselor."

Though several of the players broke down and confessed, Gandil was made of sterner stuff. When the trial ended in acquittal—crucial evidence having been destroyed by both the gamblers and the owners—he threw an all-night party at an Italian restaurant. "That'll learn [American League president] Ban Johnson he can't frame an honest bunch of ballplayers," he snarled to reporters.

Barred from ever again playing baseball, Chick Gandil made a living as a plumber. He left behind a record for greed and cynicism that today's ballplayers can only marvel at.

Warren G. Harding

HISTORIANS WILL ARGUE for hours about who was our best president, but there is no such disagreement about who was our worst. Warren G. Harding was a small-town newspaper publisher and professional backslapper who made speeches that were as mellifluous as a steam calliope and about as profound. In 1916 he was catapulted from the Marion, Ohio, Elks lodge into the United States Senate chambers by the unfathomable mysteries of state politics. When present on the Senate floor—he was absent 43 percent of the time—Harding whiled away the hours writing sixty-page love letters to his mistress, but never mind that. With his vacuous grin and whisky-jug bonhomie, Harding was the ideal straw man.

In 1920, Fortune smiled on this amicable mediocrity with the boom-ta-rah-rah intellect. The Republican National Convention had got itself hopelessly deadlocked. As the delegates sweltered in 102-degree heat, a cabal of reactionary senators and oil lobbyists met in the "smoke-filled room" of legend and dealed and dickered into the small hours of the morning. The conclusion they reached surprised even them. The only way out of the impasse was Warren G. Harding, Ohio's favorite son and a 20-to-1 long shot. He was everyone's second choice. Like Malvolio, Harding had greatness thrust upon him.

Harding wanted to be remembered as the president who returned the country to something he called "normalcy." Instead, he is remembered for leading it into something called "Teapot Dome," an example of official corruption unequaled until the Watergate years. Masking the venality was a presidential style that was as casual as an afternoon at the ball park. The White House staff, accustomed to the dignified formality of the Wilson years, must have thought they were hearing things when Harding ordered spittoons placed in the Oval Office, toothpicks on the

Warren G. Harding

state dinner table, and bootleg whisky in his desk drawer. The insouciance carried over into foreign affairs. Typical of Harding's conduct of foreign policy was his signing the termination of the state of war with Germany while playing golf.

Befuddled by affairs of state, Harding was at his best dealing poker to his cabinet officers, pumping the hands of White House tourists, or making love to his mistress in a coat closet. The best feature of his administration was its brevity. Harding died in office in 1923. It was rumored that his wife poisoned him to prevent his impeachment.

"Dr." John Brinkley

"ARE YOU A MANLY MAN full of vigor?" asked the advertisements of "Dr." John Brinkley. If the answer was no, not to worry, there was a cure. For a mere $750, Brinkley would give you the transplanted glands of a billy goat. Rejuvenation was guaranteed. Brinkley had discovered the secret of eternal youth that had eluded Ponce de León.

Brinkley developed his glandular theories while working for the meat-packing firm of Swift & Co. After two months in the army, one month of which was spent under psychiatric observation, he established the Brinkley Gland Hospital in Milford, Kansas. The goats were kept in a pen in the backyard so that patients could personally select their capric donors, like diners at a lobster house.

Business boomed. Denim-clad old ganders were soon proclaiming themselves spry as barnyard roosters. The Maharaja Thakou of Morvi came all the way from India for the transplant.

The publisher of the *Los Angeles Times* was so pleased with the operation that he gave Brinkley free advertising space in his paper. Goats hadn't been this much in the news since Nijinsky wiggled and writhed in *L'Après-midi d'un faune*. By 1923 Brinkley had become what the AMA described as a "giant in quackery."

He had also become a multimillionaire who owned a fleet of Cadillacs, a plane, a yacht, and his own radio station whose signal could easily be heard in the middle of the Atlantic Ocean. "Friends," cooed the soothing voice on KFKB, "don't let the roaring twenties roar by you. Come to Milford and recharge those batteries. A man is only as old as his glands. And friends, don't forget our contest. You can win five hundred dollars for most successfully completing the sentence, 'Dr. Brinkley is the world's foremost surgeon because . . .' "

By 1930, Brinkley was thinking big. He ran for governor with the slogan, "Let's Pasture the Goats on the Statehouse Lawn." Newspaper editors fretted, "Shall Kansans be greeted by a jibing ba-a-a as they walk the streets of other states?" Despite assurances from his astrologer that he would win, Brinkley was beaten by Alf Landon. Evidently the defeat soured him on democracy, for his subsequent political efforts were devoted to bankrolling the Silver Shirt movement of William Dudley Pelley, the Indiana Nazi.

After a long battle, Brinkley was finally shut down by the AMA and forced to move his outfit to Mexico. He died in 1942 of a heart attack after Mexican authorities tore down his transmitter.

"Dr." John Brinkley

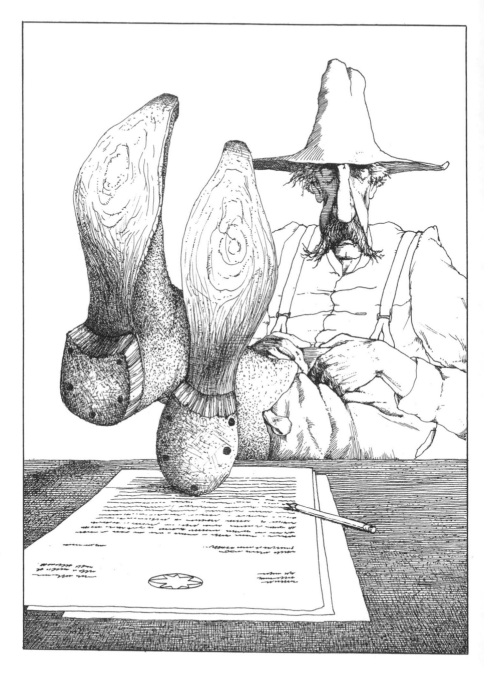

Alfalfa Bill Murray

Alfalfa Bill Murray

WHEN WILLIAM "ALFALFA BILL" MURRAY became Governor of Oklahoma in 1930, demagoguery had its finest hour.

Like most Dogpatch-style politicians, Murray made his appeal to the "plain folks." His gubernatorial campaign had more hokum and ballyhoo than a barn dance. "I will plow straight furrows and blast all stumps," he said on the hustings. "The common people and I can lick the whole lousy gang." If elected, he would call an "open season on millionaires." "Pour it on, Bill!" howled the rustics. "Wal, when Bill gits out thar in thet capitol house, he's a-gonna rare back on his hind legs an' git the job did lak it oughter be did, heh?"

Hardly. Elected to represent the common man, Murray was an uncommonly bad governor. He had promised to abolish the patronage system, but the payroll swelled with relatives and friends, including a chauffeur who was appointed director of the state institute for the feebleminded. He had promised to put an end to the wholesale pardoning of prisoners, but 542 were released during his first year alone. Alfalfa Bill bypassed the legislature and judiciary and governed by executive order, calling out the National Guard when necessary. He placed the oil fields under martial law and named his cousin "generalissimo" of the occupying troops. The federal government withdrew relief funds from his control, charging incompetent administration. Rumblings of impeachment were heard, but Alfalfa Bill hung on. "If the legislature attempts to impeach me," he drawled, "it'll be like a bunch of jackrabbits trying to pull a wildcat out of a tree."

He propped up his sagging popularity by holding square dances in the executive mansion and planting potatoes in its garden. He called for legislation punishing "high-toned bums" who refused to conform to the "overall standard." He threatened to "throw a bomb into the state's educational system." As far as Alfalfa Bill was concerned, if a little learning was a dangerous thing, a lot of it was an outright conspiracy.

Turned out of office in 1934, Murray retired to a hotel room in Tishomingo to lick his wounds, write his memoirs, and annoy his landlady by spitting tobacco juice on the carpet. His forages into the rangelands of belles-lettres include an essay on race relations entitled *The Negro's Place in the Call of Race,* and the dispiriting valedictory, *Uncle Sam Needs a Dictator.*

ℳa Barker

"THE FAMILY THAT SLAYS TOGETHER stays together" was Ma Barker's motto. Her boys—Herman, Red, Doc, and Freddie—began stealing when they were old enough to walk away with the goods. When they were caught, Ma gave them quite a scolding, not for stealing but for being apprehended. Then, in the patient, understanding way of all mothers, she showed them how it should have been done.

The boys learned quickly and soon commanded a small army of juvenile delinquents. The gang met in the Barker house, Ma presiding like some demonic cub scout den mother. She brought them along carefully. They had to learn how to steal hubcaps before they could steal the rest of the car. Gradually, slingshots gave way to machine guns, candy stores to banks. When kidnapping came into vogue after the Lindbergh case, that too was added to their repertoire. They murdered as casually as other families picnicked. With Ma and the boys, the nuclear family reached critical mass.

They cut a swath of mayhem rumbling about the dust bowls

Ma Barker

of the Depression in a stolen DeSoto. The deadly music of the instruments they carried in violin cases was heard from Minnesota to Oklahoma. One victim was an attorney whose legal performance had failed to impress Ma. Another was a doctor who had promised to remove Freddie's fingerprints with hydrochloric acid and a mechanical pencil sharpener. Yet another was one of Ma's lovers, whom she suspected of being a police spy.

The gang metastasized to thirty-five hoodlums in a dozen states. But as membership in the club increased, Ma's control over it weakened. It was no longer *en famille.* One by one the gang members were picked off, arrested, or turned into informants. Loyalty was not a Barker strong suit.

Herman, a high-strung boy, blew his brains out after being foiled in a burglary. Doc was sent to Alcatraz and died trying to escape. Red drew a twenty-five-year stretch at Leavenworth. By 1935, only Ma and Freddie remained. They fled to Florida and for a few months enjoyed a tropical vacation. Their favorite form of play was to cruise through the swamps in a motorboat, machine-gunning alligators. They met a similar fate themselves when FBI agents disguised as fishermen surrounded their bungalow and ventilated it with 1,500 rounds of ammunition. Ma and her boys are buried in a family plot in Welch, Oklahoma, three hundred feet from their nearest neighbor.

Wilbur Glenn Voliva

WILBUR GLENN VOLIVA offered $5,000 to anyone who could disprove his theory that the world was flat. "The earth is like a pie pan," he postulated in 1926, "with the North Pole at the center. Why, if the world were round the Australians, who are underneath us according to all astronomers, would have to have hooks on their feet to keep from falling off."

Voliva commanded that his theory be taught in the local schools. He wielded absolute authority as "General Overseer" of Zion, a fundamentalist community located north of Chicago. His blue laws were as surprising as his scientific ideas. Even a Moral Majoritarian would have blinked at sight of the Zion Guard, a crack religious police force who toted Bibles in their belts and wore caps inscribed with PATIENCE. Spitting and swearing could land you in jail. A cigarette was likely to be plucked from your lips and crushed under a Zion Guard boot. Many a Sunday tourist had spent the afternoon in jail after being arrested for whistling. Banned from the streets of Zion were pork products, oysters, doctors, and tan shoes. Voliva suggested that ladies in high heels be placed in insane asylums.

But to return to his main fixation, he was so convinced the world was flat that he made several trips around it to promulgate his theory. "I can whip to smithereens any man in the world in a mental battle," he shouted. "I have never met a professor or student who knew a millionth as much on any subject as I do." Astronomers were nothing more than "poor, ignorant, conceited fools." Audiences sat dumbfounded as Voliva spoke:

"The idea of a sun millions of miles in diameter and ninety-one million miles away is silly. The sun is only thirty-two miles across and is not more than three thousand miles from earth. It stands to reason that it must be so. God made the sun to light the earth and therefore must have placed it close to the task it was

Wilbur Glenn Voliva

designed to do. What would you think of a man who built a house in Zion, and put the lamp to light it in Kenosha, Wisconsin?"

Although he predicted that he would live to 120 on a diet of Brazil nuts and buttermilk, Voliva died in 1942 at age 77. The $5,000 reward was never collected.

Brigadier General Herbert C. Holdridge

BRIGADIER GEN. HERBERT C. HOLDRIDGE was convinced it was his destiny to become president of the United States.

In 1952 he planned to use "dark-horse stalking tactics" as the candidate for the American Vegetarian party, but like so many well-laid plans of mice and men, this came to nothing. Four years later, Prohibition Party leader Enoch Hardwick asked him to be his running mate and Holdridge accepted the Veep slot. After all, he reasoned, Hardwick was seventy-four years old and probably wouldn't live to complete his term. But once again Holdridge tasted the gall of defeat.

In 1959, he tried another tack. Alongside Chief Mad Bear Anderson he campaigned for the establishment of a separate Indian nation in the State of New York. Although this goal also eluded him, there was some consolation. For his efforts he was initiated into the Wolf Clan of the Mohawk Nation and given the name BA-HA-RHE-WHE-HA-WHE ("Bringing a Message").

In 1960, he hit the presidential warpath with a whoop and a

holler, leading an outfit calling themselves the Minutemen of the Constitution. When John F. Kennedy was elected instead, Holdridge began to sense a conspiracy. He declared that Kennedy had "usurped" the Oval Office and was putting into place a "theocratic dictatorship" engineered by the Federal Reserve System and the Vatican. Holdridge knew what he had to do. Drastic action was called for. Pronouncing the federal government null and void, he replaced it with the Constitutional Provisional Government of the United States or, as he sometimes called it, OOH-N-GWE-HOO-WHE ("True Americans"). He named himself chief magistrate.

"You are directed to make an immediate arrest of John F. Kennedy, this individual who is clearly insane," he wrote to J. Edgar Hoover on CPGUS stationery. He described how Kennedy, "in conspiracy with the Pope of the Roman Catholic Church," had betrayed the country to NATO, "the revived Holy Roman Empire."

CPGUS was run out of Holdridge's house in Southern California. And it was no easy thing. Constantly on the alert for the assassins dispatched by the CIA, the FBI, the Vatican, and the Post Office, Holdridge also had to fight off efforts to have him declared a mental incompetent. Nonetheless, Holdridge remained optimistic. "I have it on sound spiritual authority," he announced, "that I am soon going to walk into the top office—which I already hold legally—and take over without firing a shot."

Brigadier General Herbert C. Holdridge

Joe Pyne

Joe Pyne

CALLING THE "Joe Pyne Show" a talk show is like calling the Spanish Inquisition a question-and-answer session. It would be better described as the public stocks in the electronic global village. In 1966, at the height of the show's popularity, millions of people in 254 cities tuned in every Saturday night to watch the impromptu Theater of Cruelty. Why pay to see *Who's Afraid of Virginia Woolf?* or *Marat/Sade* when you can watch Joe Pyne for free? "This is a fist-in-the-mouth as opposed to a tongue-in-the-cheek show," said Joe. "My guests know they are going to be in a fight." Said his producer, "We want emotion, not mental involvement."

An ex-marine who had won three battle stars and lost one leg, Joe Pyne had the interviewing grace of a drill instructor. "Just why do you think people should feel sorry for you?" he demanded of an epileptic guest. "You're sputtering like an old Ford," he told one who was stammering, "go gargle with razor blades." Sometimes his guests were so rattled they became unglued. "That's the only time I feel helpless," said the host, "when they start crying." Occasionally a guest would blurt out terrible secrets. One man, for example, confessed to being a Peeping Tom.

What sort of people appeared on Joe's Roman Circus? The favorites were Nazis, prophets of free LSD, pornographers, ex-mental patients, hucksters of every stripe, and people who claimed they were passing through earth on their way to other planets. It wasn't exactly the "MacNeil-Lehrer Report." "I have no respect for anyone who appears on my show," said Joe. "It's a masochism syndrome. They look to me for approbation, as a father image, but sometimes they feel the need to be punished and they know I'll punish them." After Joe had finished "interviewing" a guest, he threw the carcass to the audience, who shouted

77

insults and inanities from a "beef box."

Images filter back through the years. Remember the time an angry guest threw a telephone at Joe? Or the time Joe's sidekick, Ozzie Whiffletree, was punched in the nose? How about the time during the Watts riots when Joe waved a pistol at a black guest and said he knew what he'd do if a rioter came near him?

Tough marine that he was, Joe refused to give up smoking. "I'd rather take a chance than be a fat neurotic," he growled through a cloud of cigarette fumes. Joe Pyne died of cancer in 1970 at age forty-four.

DATE DUE